CCSS Genre Folktale

 Y0-BBD-650

Essential Question
What are some messages in animal stories?

The Cockroach and the Mouse

by Julia Wall
illustrated by Tim Jones

Chapter 1

Something Round and Silver

Martina Cockroach was cleaning her house when a shiny object **attracted** her attention. She saw something round and silver stuck in the floorboards.

"What is that?" Martina muttered as she looked more closely.

Martina pulled and tugged at the round silver thing until suddenly it popped out.

The silver thing **wobbled** around wildly and made a noise like a drum roll. Then it stopped moving.

Martina crept closer and exclaimed, "It's a coin!"

She was lucky to have such good **fortune**. Then Martina had an idea. Maybe she could use her new treasure to help her get something that she wanted.

"I can use the coin to help me choose a husband," Martina thought. She had four **suitors**, and she couldn't decide which one to marry.

Martina's suitors loved corn cakes, called arepas. "I will use the coin to buy *arepas*, because the delicious smell will attract my suitors," Martina said.

Then Martina thought about what she would wear to attract her suitors. She chose a red dress made of silk **fabric**.

STOP AND CHECK

What does clever Martina decide to do with the coin?

Chapter 2

Martina Buys Corn Cakes

The next morning, Martina put on her red dress, took the silver coin and set out for the bakery. Her **progress** through the streets was slow because the coin was very heavy.

At last, Martina arrived at the bakery and **requested** five arepas. She gave the baker the silver coin.

The arepas were warm, and they smelled good. "I would like to eat one now," Martina thought. But she **controlled** her **greed** and made herself wait for the suitors.

Martina went home and put the arepas on the table on the patio. Then she sat down and waited for her suitors to smell the arepas.

STOP AND CHECK

Why doesn't Martina eat an arepa right away?

Chapter 3

Martina Has Visitors

Martina didn't have to wait long before Goat smelled the arepas, and soon he arrived at Martina's house. He said, "You look **dazzling** today, Martina. What's that delicious smell?" Goat **smacked** his lips loudly.

"Arepas," Martina replied. "You must sing to me. If I like your song, you may have an arepa *and* you may ask me to marry you."

"Bleat! Bleeaatt! Bleat, bleeaatt!" Goat sang.

Martina covered her ears, crying, "Stop, Goat!" She decided to be **honest** and said, "Your singing hurts my ears."

"Does that mean that I can't have an arepa?" asked Goat.

"You can't have an arepa, and you can't marry me," said Martina. Goat **trudged** away sadly.

When Cat arrived next, Martina told him about her plan for choosing a husband.

"Meow! Mee-oww!" Cat whined.

Martina thought his voice was terrible. "No arepas for you, Cat. And I'm not going to marry you," she said.

Rooster was Martina's third suitor.

"I sing every morning," he said proudly. "I'm sure you'll like my song."

Martina thought that sounded promising.

"COCK-A-DOODLE-DOO!" crowed Rooster.

"Rooster, you frightened me!" said Martina.

"My song is meant to wake everyone up," said Rooster.

"No one could sleep through that noise!" said Martina. She wouldn't marry Rooster.

Perez the Mouse was the last suitor to arrive. He began to sing.

"Cucarachita Martina,
No cockroach is sweeter.
I would lose my whiskers for you,
If that was what I had to do!"

Perez's voice was beautiful. Martina's heart **soared**, and she knew she had found her **match**. Her plan had worked, and she would marry Perez.

STOP AND CHECK

Why does Martina want to marry Perez?

Chapter 4   Perez Falls into the Pot

Martina invited Perez to dinner to **celebrate** their engagement. "I will make my special soup," she said to Perez.

Martina went out to buy some salt. While she was gone, Perez stirred her special soup.

Martina met Goat on the way to the store.

"You look happy, Martina," Goat said. "Who are you going to marry?"

"Perez," replied Martina, "I'm making soup. Come and eat it with us. Ask Cat and Rooster to come, too."

At Martina's house, Perez was stirring the soup. "I wonder what is in the soup," he thought. "I will take a look."

Perez stood on tiptoe, but he lost his balance and fell into the soup with a splash.

At that moment, Goat, Cat, and Rooster arrived.

"Help!" screamed Perez. "I'm in the soup!"

The three other animals looked at each other. If Perez died, one of them could marry Martina.

Then Martina came in. "Where's Perez?"

"I'm in the pot!" Perez shouted.

"Help him!" screamed Martina.

Goat, Cat, and Rooster remembered that Perez was their friend. Friends help each other out, so they pulled him out of the pot.

Perez forgave them, and the friends celebrated with hot soup and warm arepas.

STOP AND CHECK

Why don't Goat, Cat, and Rooster rescue Perez right away?

Respond to Reading

Summarize

Summarize *The Cockroach and the Mouse*. Your graphic organizer may help you.

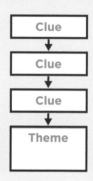

Text Evidence

1. Reread page 4. What clever thing does Martina do with the coin? THEME

2. What does the word *delicious* mean on page 4? What clues help you figure this out? VOCABULARY

3. Write about why Martina chose Perez to be her husband. Why didn't she choose the other animals? WRITE ABOUT READING

Compare Texts

Read about how Fox and Crane trick each other.

Fox and Crane

One day Fox and Crane were hunting a mouse. Fox was about to pounce on the mouse when Crane snapped her bill shut. The mouse disappeared down her throat.

"That was tasty," said Crane.

"But that mouse was my lunch!" cried Fox.

"But I caught it," replied Crane.

Fox knew Crane was right, but he had a plan to get back at her. "Come to my place tomorrow for mouse soup," he said.

Crane wondered what sneaky Fox was planning. The next day, she went to Fox's den.

Fox was making his soup.

"That smells good!" exclaimed Crane.

Fox poured the soup into two shallow bowls, and then he tasted the soup. "It's delicious!" Fox said.

Crane couldn't drink her soup because her long bill wouldn't fit into the shallow bowl. "Fox is playing a trick on me," she thought.

"This tastes different than the mouse soup I make," Crane lied. "Come and have mouse soup with me tomorrow."

Fox wondered what crafty Crane was planning.

The next day, Crane put her soup into two tall jars. Fox tried to drink from the jar. But he couldn't reach the soup. Crane and Fox laughed.

"Let's stop playing tricks on each other. We can hunt for mice and make soup together," Fox said. "I'll bring my jar!" said Crane.

"I'll bring my bowl," said Fox.

Make Connections

What do the animals in *Fox and Crane* teach us?
ESSENTIAL QUESTION

How are the endings of *The Cockroach and the Mouse* and *Fox and Crane* similar? How are they different? TEXT TO TEXT

Focus on Literary Elements

Imagery Imagery describes how something looks, sounds, smells, feels, or tastes. These images help us to understand a story better.

Read and Find In *The Cockroach and the Mouse*, the writer uses words to create imagery. The words *round*, *silver*, and *shiny* on page 2 help us to imagine the coin. On page 3, the writer uses the words *pulled*, *tugged*, and *popped*. These words help us to imagine Martina trying to get the coin out.

Your Turn

Reread page 6. Find the words that the writer uses to describe the arepas.